Heart on Your Sleeve Girl

Heart On Your Sleeve Girl

Poems by

Jennifer Taylor

Heart On Your Sleeve Girl

Published by Face Value Enterprises, Inc.
P.O. Box 7344
Northridge, CA 91327

All rights reserved. No part of this book may be reproduced or used in any form without permission from publisher.

Cover photo by Bobby Quillard

ISBN #978-1-7365999-0-7

© 2021 Face Value Enterprises, Inc.

Table of Contents

Acknowledgement	8
Introduction	10
Torn	12
What am I?	13
The Edge	14
Scarlet A	15
If I Were Red	16
Mask	17
I'll Never Learn	18
Power and Money	19
The Memory of You	20
Remember Me, My Love	21
If I Promise	22
To Be With You	23
It's Your Fault	24
I Don't Need You	25
Thinking of You	26
To Get to the Top	27
Springtime	28
In Comparison to You	29
I Love You	30
If I Could	31
The Only Thing That Matters	32
Apart	33
To My Best Friend	34
I Believe in You	35
When I Close My Eyes	36
I've Got A Lot	37
I'll Love You Forever	38
Only In You	39
Our Love Is Real	40
I'll Never Stop Loving You	41
When I Go Away	42
I Will Hurt You Never	43
Both of Us Will Win	44

I'll Wait	45
I Cry a Little Less	46
Thanksgiving Poem	47
The Love in My Heart	48
Change	49
The Rainbow in My Life	50
Behind the Wall	51
Through With You	52
Break	53
Alone	54
Again	55
Chains	56
All I Ever Need	57
Whole	58
Hope	59
Do You Believe in Destiny?	60
Close Up	61
Inspiration	62
First Time, Last Times	63-64
The Grace of God	65

Acknowledgement

Paul, it's always been you. Thank you for our two greatest gifts, Jake and Samantha. And, Jesus, thank you for all.

Introduction

Back in 2010, I was going to be included in an interview with my co stars from Two and a Half Men, and I was nervous. How was I ever going to compare to these talented, famous people?

My husband, Paul, gave me some of the best advice I've ever received. He said, "Remember, you're not witty girl, or clever girl. Don't try to be like them. You're heart on your sleeve girl. Just be yourself and you'll do great." I never did have to worry about how the interview turned out. They didn't use my clip, but the advice has served me well.

Heart on your sleeve girl. For better or for worse, it's who I am. Who I've always been. Straight forward and sentimental. Kind of like my poetry.

I started writing as a kid, but I never dared show my work to anyone. Now that I am older, I'm much less concerned with what others think. Fear of not being good enough is less important than sharing my heart. The good, bad, and ugly.

I hope these poems bring you joy, hope, or solace in sorrow. If nothing else, it's a glimpse of my heart through the years.

Thanks for taking the time to read.

-Jennifer Taylor

Torn

Torn between two
Which way should I go?
It all seems so new
It's so hard to know.

Two paths to take
Each with a different end
Decisions to make
Old wounds that must mend.

Two different feelings
Two separate hearts
Too many outcomes
And so many parts.

Torn between two
I wish there was one
Now that it's over
I'm left with none.

-March 1988

What am I?

I am more than a feeling
But not quite a fact.
My breadth exceeds all banal boundaries.
I germinate inside you
And when the time is right
I blossom into an aura of vernal radiance
Or wither into a blanket of morbid sorrow.
I can make you smile in elation
Or taste the salty tears of bitterness.
I am what this world lacks
And most people need.

-September 1988

The Edge

You're on the edge of insanity
That lonely place you thought
You'd never be
But now it's so real
And it's cold like the frostbitten sky.

Running in circles
But you can't touch base
Try to cover your eyes
But you can't feel your face
And now you're so lost
And your scared and you ask yourself why.

You stare at the line
That you can't erase
Immeasurable Time
That we can't embrace
But you've been looking so long
And so hard that you just want to die.

When you look ahead
To see your fate
The future is past
And now the present is late
But your visions are sharp
And they cut like a shard of your life.

So when you can't cope
And you want to escape
But don't want to retreat
To your callous state
Just reach for my hand
I'll be there
And I stay by your side.

-October 1988

Scarlet A

Thy heart is on display for all to see
A patch that burns within thy blackened soul
To show the deed that hath defamed thy name
They bid thee to expose the Scarlet A.
Doest thou think that they are so unaware
And do not know the priest that broke his faith?
Methinks that thou are not guilty of sin
Because thy saintly priest was there to give
The love thee were deprived from thine own mate
Hold up thy head and boast thy Scarlet A

-1988

If I Were Red...

If I were red, would you marry me?
Would you love me if my heavy burgundy curtain
Was drawn about my heart
And replaced the cherry glow of bliss
Which lightly kissed my cheeks?
And would you care if sorrow-laden eyes
Cast maroon shadows on my sallow skin
Just as if warm sparkling rubies were
Rollicking in my vivacious eyes?
Could you handle my candy apple mood
Suddenly changing into a fireball
With its blazing tongues
Searing through your soul
Like molten rock through the center of the earth
Until your crimson blood was drawn?
And can you climb over my brick wall
To behold the delicate pink roses
Without being scorched by its scalding surface?
I know you can love my blushing petals
But can you abide my sanguine thorns?

-1988

Mask

If you only knew
The face behind this mask
You'd understand my actions
You wouldn't even ask
But since I'm trapped within myself
You'll have to break the ice
You needn't use a hammer
Since I'm my only vice
When I escape this world of pain
And thaw these frozen eyes
Only then you'll understand
The truth behind the lies
So when my expression
Denies my soul
And words contradict my feelings
Try to look a little longer
And understand their meaning.

-August 1988

I'll Never Learn

I haven't learned to play life's game
With all its tricks and rules
Maybe it's because I'm too young
Or just don't have the tools.

But I haven't learned that I'm the only one I can trust
Even if they're your friend
And I haven't learned to make "friends" in high places
To get myself ahead.

I haven't learned to ignore those hurt
Or hit them while they're down
I haven't learned to cheat anyone
Not even the everyday clown.

I haven't learned to play life's game
With all its tricks and rules
And maybe if I'm lucky
I never will.

-September 1989

Power and Money

Power and money
Fortune and fame
Is that all that's important
In this opportunistic game?

Jaguars, Mercedes
Porches and Beamers
Gold plated bumpers
And monogramed mirrors.

Beverly Hills, Hollywood
Boca Raton, Rodeo Drive
Mansions worth millions
And garages built for five.

I don't understand
The purpose of these
What's so important about wealth
Tell me please.

I don't want your money
And I don't like your car
And I won't sleep in your house
Just so I can become a star.

Love and friendship
Hard work and humility
These are the things
That mean something to me.

-October 1989

The Memory of You

Even when I'm miles away
With not a soul around
I feel your presence with me
Though it does not make a sound.

I can hear your laughter
Dancing in my dreams
And I can see your smile
Shining through like beams.

And when I awake alone at night
And reach to pull you near
The feeling that you are still with me
Chases away my fear.

The memory of you washes over me
Like a shower of April rain
It fills up my emptied heart
And wipes out all my pain.

The memory of you remains with me
It lives inside my heart
I know we'll always be as one
Whether we're together or apart.

-December 1989

Remember Me, My Love

Remember me, my love
Because no one else you find
Will ever love you like I do
With their heart or with their mind.

I love you when I like you
And when I hate you
I love you even more
There is nothing you could ever do
To make me shut my door.

You hurt me time and time again
You stole my lonely heart
You came into my life and then
You tore it all apart.

I could never love another
The way that I love you
I've given you all my passion
It would hurt to much to start anew.

So remember me, my love
As I've told you once before
I love you with all my heart
And no one else could ever love you more.

-December 1989

If I Promise

If I promise you the moon
If I promise you the sea
I promise that you'll have them soon
Whatever the price may be.

If I promise you the sun
That shines so bright each day
I will not sleep until it's done
I'll give you each and every ray.

If I promise you the sky
The cloudless expanse of blue
Even if I have to lie
I swear I'll give it to you.

If I promise you the star
That I wish on every night
I'll travel though the place be far
I'll give it to you tonight.

If I promise you my love
I swear I will be true
Though everything else may fade away
My heart will always belong to you.

-December 1989

To Be With You

I could find a richer man
And probably better looking too
But I wouldn't give him a second glance
If I knew I was loved by you.

I could be a movie star
And have my very own crew
But I'd give up every claim to fame
Only to be with you.

I could be a millionaire
And have everything I owned be brand new
But I'd lose all my money and live on the street
If anyone ever tried to hurt you.

If you were damned to hell
Never again to see skies of blue
I'd gladly turn my back on heaven
Just to spend my life with you.

There are lots of things that I could be
And better things to do
But none of it would mean very much to me
If I couldn't be with you.

-January 1990

It's Your Fault

With a touch you can make me happy
With a word you can make me sad
At your whim you control my feelings
And every emotion I've ever had.

When you find something funny
It's me who has the smile
And when something upsets you
It's my tears that stain the tile.

You are the key to my happiness
And you are the cause of my pain
So in everything that I may do
You are the one to blame.

My emotions no longer belong to me
They are an extension of yours
You can choose to open up my heart
Or you can lock its doors.

I don't want to surrender to you
All the freedom I once had
But you've broken all my defenses
And now the cards are in your hand.

Well now you know what you do to me
Believe me when I say its true
You own my heart and what you do now
Is entirely up to you.

-January 1990

I Don't Need You

I don't need your warm, sweet voice
To help me fall asleep
And I don't need your big, strong arms
Around me when I weep.

I don't need your sunny smile
To get me through the day
And I don't need your soothing words
To keep my fears at bay.

I don't need your soft caress
To get me through the night
And I don't need your tender kiss
Or for you to hold me tight.

I don't need your body
I don't need your soul
And I don't need your love
To make me feel whole.

I don't need to tell you
That none of this is true
No matter how I try to deny it
I can't help but need you.

-January 1990

Thinking of You

It's only been a couple of days
Since we were last together
But even when it's just a day
It seems to last forever.

Every minute that we're apart
I play inside my mind
Every word that you have said
Whether it was cruel or kind.

Even when I sleep at night
I see you in my dreams
There's not a moment I don't think of you
At least that's how it seems.

No matter what I'm doing
I always think of you
When I should be doing something else
You enter my thoughts on cue

I think about you all the time
And on my mind you'll always be
I wish I knew that this was how much
You always thought of me.

-January 1990

To Get To The Top

You can claw your way to the top
In your quest for fortune and fame
But I won't fight to be number one
To me it's all just the same.

You can be bitchy to everyone else
But to the clients be dripping with honey
But I won't kiss ass if they're not nice to me
Being two-faced is not worth the money.

You can screw any big shot you please
Just to get their connections
But I'd much rather be just plain ole me
Than dishonest with my affections.

After your up on the top of the world
And look down at the people you stepped on
Take a good look around and I'm sure you will find
That the friends you once had are now all gone.

If fame and fortune is to happen to me
I will not be desperate to get there
I'll just take my time and if it's meant to be
I won't have to be cruel or unfair.

It may take me longer to get to the top
But at least I'll never have had to be
A bitch and a whore who used everyone else
Because I'll always have been true to me.

-January 1990

Springtime

Today's the day; the first day of spring
And everything seems brand new
To some it may not seem a big thing
But it makes me think of you.

When the robin sings his high-pitch song
At the beginning of the day
I hear your sweet voice inside my head
And all the beautiful things you say.

When the bright red rose awakes from sleep
And blinds me with its grace
The only image that enters my mind
Is the radiance of your face.

When the golden-red sun breaks the dawn
And scatters its warming light
I only feel the heat of your body
Next to mine in the middle of the night.

When the gentle showers of springtime fall
And dampen my upturned face
The only thing I really feel
Is the strength of your embrace.

When the mystical rainbow chases the clouds
Though it only stays but a while
When I look to the sky I only see
The magic of your smile.

Springtime's my favorite part of the year
For it makes me think of you dear
But know this without any reason
That I love you every day of every season.

-March 1990

In Comparison To You

I could compare you to the deep blue sea
And the tide that ebbs and flows
Or the gentle waves that roll to shore
That grow stronger when the sea wind blows.

And I could compare you to the bright blue sky
With scattered clouds of billowing white
Or the radiant light of the millions of stars
That shine on the darkest of nights.

Or I could compare you to the morning sun
That rises up each day
And spreads around its warming light
With every golden ray.

I can compare you to anything
And here I only named a few
But there is nothing that I can compare
To how I feel when I'm with you.

-March 1990

I Love You

I don't think I could ever count
The reasons I love you
There are lots of them that I could name
Like things you say or do.

But there are many more I can't explain
No matter how I try
To say there is one simple reason
Would only be a lie.

I love you because you made me happy
When you came into my life
You placed a song within my heart
That makes me feel alive.

I love you because of who you are
And there's only one of you
You're special to me in every way
And no one else will ever do.

I don't know what you did to me
To make me feel this way
But whatever spell you cast on me
I don't want it to go away.

I could write about you forever
And every word would be true
But it would only touch the surface
Of how much I really love you.

-April 1990

If I Could

It hurts to see you hurt so bad
Although it never happened to me
I feel the pain you're going through
And how hard for you it must be.

I know I can't heal your wounds
Or wipe away your tears
The only thing that can do that
Is the passing of the years.

But if there is anything I can do
To make your sorrow less
Just tell me what it is
I'd do anything to give you a moment of happiness.

If there was anyway I could
I'd give up everything and set you free
So you could have her back again
If it would make you happy.

I can't be happy when you are sad
And although it won't take away your pain
I want to tell you I love you
Again and again and again.

-April 1990

The Only Thing That Really Matters

You're the only thing that really matters
When I sit and think things through
Because everything would mean nothing to me
If I didn't have you.

The only thing that really matters
Is the trust that we both share
Because to have faith in someone totally
Truly is quite rare.

The only thing that really counts
Is the love that you give me
And that's more special than any gift
That I will ever receive.

The only thing that has any meaning
Is the joy you have placed in my heart
You are the definition of happiness
And I felt it right from the start.

You're the only thing that really matters
Because you're the only thing I need
You're the only one I truly love
And you mean everything to me.

-May 1990

If We're Apart

If ever we are apart
Across the seas of blue
Not even a thousand oceans
Could take me away from you.

And I might fall asleep in another land
Without you next to me
But I'll still feel your arms draw me in close
Because in my heart is where you'll be.

There won't be a single moment
When I'm not missing you
But knowing that you'll be waiting for me
Is enough to get me through.

I love you more than I can say
Or I can even do
But I really have to let you know
I'm truly in love with you.

-June 1990

To My Best Friend

Whenever we're together
I put everything out of mind
Because nothing else really matters
When you are by my side.

Our love is very special
Because it's so hard to find
Two people who love as honestly
And wholly as you and I.

If we were any closer
We surely would be one
You have already become a part of me
And we've only just begun.

Even when we argue
I'll still be loving you
And it will only make us closer
Because our love will bring us through.

I know I've said I love you
So many times before
But my feeling have grown stronger
And I mean it even more.

So I'll tell you again I love you
And I hope that you can see
The only thing I'll ever need
Is you always loving me.

-June 1990

I Believe in You

I don't care who you are
Or what you choose to do
When I told you I loved you
I meant I'll always love you.

As long as you really think you're right
And believe in whatever you do
I'll be there right by your side
Because I believe in you.

Even if the odds are against you
One hundred thousand to one
I'll still be there to cheer for you
If you think it could be done.

Even if you were convicted for murder
And the gun was found in your hand
If you said you were innocent
I'd gladly take the stand.

As long as you like yourself
And believe in what you do
It doesn't matter what others say
Because I'll always have respect for you.

Even if I don't agree
With some of the things you do
I'll stick by your side and love you the same
Because I believe in you.

-June 1990

When I Close My Eyes

When I close my eyes
I see your face
And it gives me a smile
That I can't erase.
I hear your voice
Inside my head
And every beautiful word
That you have said.
I smell your body
When it's soaking wet
After we make love
And it's sweet from sweat.
I taste your lips
And I can't define
How good it feels
When they are next to mine.
I feel your love
And it makes me wise
Because it still feels strong
When I close my eyes.

-June 1990

I've Got a Lot

I might not have lots of money
Or drive a very nice car
And I have to make a living
Working in a seedy little bar.

I know I've got lots of problems
With solutions that are hard to find
And everything that I am afraid of
Is all within my mind.

But to me I've got
The world at my feet
Because I've got things
That can't be beat.

I've got someone who loves me
Because I am me
And we both trust each other
So honestly.

I can do without those material things
Because God gave me the hope
To believe things will get better
And gave me a love
That can last forever.

-July 1990

I Love You Forever

Even though we sometimes fight
And get upset too
I'll never really be able to express
Truly how much I love you.

Just the tiniest words you say to me
Or the smallest things you do
Helps me put life back into perspective
And stops me from feeling blue.

I truly would be lost without you
You've helped me set sight on a goal
And I know with your help it will someday come true
Although lately it has been on hold.

I've never felt this way before
So everything feels brand new
But I know that I'll love you now and forever
And that's my most sincere promise to you.

I'd hurt myself before I ever tried to hurt you
And I never will be untrue
I need you with every grain of my heart
Because I am forever in love with you.

-July 1990

Only In You

All the gold-drenched rays of the morning light
come only from the sun.
And all the white-hot brightness of the midnight stars
are only found in the sky.
All the vibrant flowers and lush green fields
come only from one earth.
And all of the love, happiness, and trust in my life
I only found in you.

-July 1990

Our Love Is Real

I love it when you hold me close
With your arms around me tight
When we are together
In the middle of the night.

And I love it when you don't touch me
But caress my with your gaze
You can see right through to me
And set my heart ablaze.

I love it when you treat me sweet
And talk to me so gentle
You make me feel as if I am
A rose's delicate petal.

But I love it when you play with me
And we wrestle on the floor
It proves to us we're also friends
And we like each other even more.

I love it when we tell each other
Exactly how we feel
And because we take the bad with good
It makes our love so real.

-July 1990

I'll Never Stop Loving You

When the sun ceases to shine
And the sky is no longer blue
When the winds forget to blow
That's when I'll stop loving you.

When every mountain crumbles
And the stars are forever out of view
When all the oceans are drained
That's when I'll stop loving you.

When all the birds stop singing
And the rain stops falling too
When the swan leaves its mate
That's when I'll stop loving you.

When all of these things happen
Not one or even two
When the earth is torn asunder
That's when I'll stop loving you.

None of these may happen
But even if they do
I'll love you after I am gone
Because I will never stop loving you.

-August 1990

When I Go Away

Every time I go away
And have to say good-bye
It doesn't matter how short the stay
It always makes me cry.

A part of me is missing
When I'm not with you
There's a hollow feeling deep inside
That makes me feel so blue.

The time we spend together
I cherish more than life
And when we are apart
It cuts just like a knife.

I never will get used to
Being away from you
But even through the distance
I know our love is true.

My love is an endless river
That runs straight through my heart
And even when we're not together
Nothing could ever tear our love apart.

-August 1990

I Will Hurt You Never

I'm sorry if what you said upset me
But I'm trying to make you see
I know you didn't mean to do it
But you really did hurt me.

I know that you've been hurt before
And are afraid to get too close
But can't you see that I'm not her
And I live in the shadow of her ghost.

When I say that I won't hurt you
I wish you'd believe it's true
I know that actions speak louder than words
But everything I do is for you.

I know that only time
Will make you totally trust me
But I want you to know that I'll be here
Although I may be in agony.

I'll try to keep my distance
So you can think things through
And even though it upsets me
I'll happily wait for you.

The feelings you are having now
Just tear my soul apart
But I will be here waiting for you
Because you have control of my heart.

Please remember when I said to you
I love you dear forever
I also made a sincere promise
That I would hurt you never.

-September 1990

Both of Us Will Win

I know that you are drawing back
So you can protect your heart
But how will you know if I will break it
If we are always are apart.

There's not a thing I want from you
I only want your love
My love for you is innocent
The wings of a snow white dove.

I hope you soon will understand
That my love for you is true
And hurting you is something
I honestly would never do.

I wish that you would take the chance
And let me in your heart again
I risked it all when I gave you my heart
But I haven't stopped letting you in.

When I promised you my heart
And said I'd always be true
I meant it and I'll be here by your side
Until you sort things through.

Nothing can make me stop loving you
Not even the pain I'm in
I know that if I'm patient
Both of us will surely win.

-September 1990

I'll Wait

I don't care
How much love it takes
For you to lower your wall
And pull off the brakes.

I'll just keep giving
All my love to you
And hope that you'll take it
And give some back too.

It doesn't matter
If it takes a long time
For you to give me your heart
Like I gave you mine.

I know that you love me
But need to be sure
That I won't steal your heart
Then run out the door.

I'll just keep my love
Waiting for you
Because soon enough
You'll see our love is true.

-October 1990

I Cry A Little Less

I remember a while ago
When there was a time
That the littlest thing you did to upset me
Would always make me cry.

I know that things are different now
And we haven't been at our best
But every time you hurt me more
I cry a little less.

When you forget the plans we've made
Although I feel depressed
Every time you forget me more
I cry a little less.

When you stay out and drink all night
So your friends will be impressed
Every time you don't come home
I cry a little less.

Whenever you don't listen to me
And think what I say is meaningless
Every time you ignore me more
I cry a little less.

Whenever I try to make things better
But end up feeling useless
Every time things go wrong
I cry a little less.

Before things start to get much worse
And I'm heading for the door
Maybe you could hurt me less
So I can feel a little more.

- November 1990

Thanksgiving Poem

I want to thank God for many things
Like for giving us this food
But mostly I am thankful
For Him giving me you.

I also want to thank you today
For giving me your love
I love you and I want you to know
You're all I'm thinking of.

Thank you for putting up with me
When I get a little crazy
Sometimes I need to step back and look
When things start getting hazy.

Thank you for being there for me
And holding me close at night
Thank you for really caring for me
And making everything seem all right.

Thank you for holding my hand when we walk
And giving me lots of kisses
Thank you for being the one that I love
And the reason for my wishes.

Thank you for being everything to me
The list could never end
But mainly I wanted to tell you today
Thank you for being my friend.

-November 1990

The Love In My Heart

If there cannot be Heaven
If there is no Hell;
Nor some things right
And not some things wrong;
And if we cannot know happiness
Without feeling sadness;
Nor understand light
Without the dark;
Then we cannot have change
Without the steadfast love
For you in my heart.

-January 1991

Change

There always comes
That eventual stage
When things get comfortable
Everything must change.

We get no fair warning
No prophets reveal
That change is soon coming
It's something you feel.

It sneaks up behind us
While we're fast asleep
It wells up inside us
And then makes us weep.

It may be for better
It may be for worse
We don't know the outcome
And we can't rehearse.

Change is something
We must learn to accept
Because we often get
What we don't expect.

When change comes around
We have to believe
Good will come of it
Although we may grieve.

-January 1990

The Rainbow in My Life

Whenever I'm down and feeling my worst
You make me feel like a queen
You make me smile and tell me that things
Aren't as bad as they seem.
When my days are gray
And filled with clouds
That will only cause me more pain
The sunshine inside you
Brightens my day
Because you are the rainbow in my life.

Whenever I'm happy and feeling my best
I owe it all to you
You are the one who cases the darkness away
And change my skies to blue
All paths lead to you
You are my pot of gold
Being with you makes everything right
Because you are the rainbow in my life.

-March 1991

Behind the Wall

She's a scared little girl
Crying in the dark, clawing at the walls
Begging for help
But no one hears her
And rarely sees her
And nobody know she's lying on the floor
Close to the edge of never coming back.

She's also a hardened woman
With broken dreams and a broken heart
No one touches her, keeping guard
With her razor sharp tongue
Sarcastic and jaded
She let's no one in
To rescue the troubled child.

So nobody know there's a dying soul
Groping for a grain of hope
Or a glimpse of light
To making living worthwhile.

-August 1991

Through With You

I've done everything that I possibly could
To get you to be mine
But I've come to realize that you do me no good
And you've finally run out of time.

You hurt me time and time again
You walked all over my heart
You think that I'll take anything
And now it's time for a fresh start.

I'm not going to wait for you to see
What you should already know
I'm tired of all of your lies and your games
And now I can let you go.

You took my love for granted
One too many times
You thought that I would wait forever
Well, now I'm saying good-bye.

I know I deserve to be happy
But you only make me cry
After everything we've been through
I still don't understand why.

I gave you a love that was honest and good
I gave you a heart that was true
You dragged me through hell and back again
And now I am through with you.

-March 1992

Break

The day you left me all alone
I cried, then turned my heart to stone.

I built the walls around me high
And let all the feelings in me die.

But sometimes when it's late at night
And all my locks are bolted tight.

I hear the tapping at my door
Of who I used to be before.

It stirs up feelings from some past
Of long before that did not last.

Someone cut me open please
So I can drain this love disease.

If I'm ever to be free
Break these walls and let me bleed.

-September 1992

Alone

I wish I could forget you
For what you've done to me
But since I know I hate you
I can't count myself as free.

I know that you once loved me
As much as I love you
I guess that's why I can't believe
The two of us are through.

I don't know why I'm holding on
To the love that we once shared
I must still think you're the only one
That ever really cared.

All my dreams are empty
All my hearts desires gone
All my faith in love has left me
All except for one.

It's sleeping in a darkened corner
Of my frozen heart
It hides behind an icy door
Never again to depart.

It tried to surface long ago
And make itself be known
But then you left
And once again
I was all alone.

-December 1992

Again

My heart is cold
It's ice and stone
It holds the only
Dream I've known.
So please don't touch me
Leave me alone.
If you get much closer
I think I'll burn.
I'll burn and then the ice
Will melt
And all the rocks will tumble
The only thing that will be left
Is my heart's true desire.
My heart's desire is for you
You'll see it honest and exposed
And then you'll break it.
Again.

-1993

Chains

I wish that I could get back to
The way I used to be
A girl who lived to laugh and love
A heart so strong and free.

But somewhere down life's lonesome road
I lost my childhood dream
Reality tore my world apart
And left me shivering in a scream.

I have this ache that's in my heart
A pain too deep for tears
An emptiness within my soul
That grows colder by the years.

I'm trapped within a shattered heart
A darkened corner of my soul
The place where lonely tears begin
And fear regains control.

Old memories claim my broken heart
While anger runs through my veins
Sorrow clouds my sightless eyes
And forgotten love keeps me in chains.

-April 1993

All I Ever Need

All I ever needed
Was to be in love with you
To be the only one you loved
And give you a heart that was true.

All I ever wanted
Was to be someone special in your life
To be the only one you trusted
The one you wanted to make your wife.

But the only thing I got from you
Were the lies that you told me
The broken heart you left me with
Every time you set me free.

So now I know that it's over
And I should have know from the start
You never intended to love me
You just played with my broken heart.

-August 1993

Whole

Have you ever felt so lonely
Have you ever felt confused
Have you ever felt so lost and cold
Unloved and abused?

I'm not sure what I am feeling now
My head's all in a daze
My life is so messed up right now
A rat trapped in a maze.

How can I ever get back to
The girl I used to be
I want to learn to laugh again
I want someone to love me.

I need to find some peace again
I need to have a goal
I need to feel important somehow
Can I once again feel whole?

-June 1994

Hope

It seems like a million years
Since I haven't been afraid
To hope or dream of having
Love in my life again.

I thought I'd live forever in fear
of truly finding happiness
I only knew the pain
that filled my heart with sadness.

But you've opened up my eyes
To see how much you care
And you've woken up my heart
And taught me how to share.

You've given my lips a reason to smile
And my eyes a light to shine
My heart now has a song to sing
To the world that you are mine.

My life again has purpose
My step now has a spring
My minds without a doubt
We are forever meant to be.

-1995

Do You Believe in Destiny?

Do you think our souls are only
half complete and that we'll
search the whole world through
until we find the other half
our perfect mate.
I believe in destiny.
I believe I am blessed to have found another person
who complements my strengths
and diminishes my weaknesses
Someone who opens up my eyes
and takes hold of my heart
Someone who gives me solid ground to stand on
But wings to let me soar.
Someone who gives my heart a reason to beat from day to day.
Yes, I believe in destiny.
Do you?

-December 1995

Close Up

Your eye catches mine
and my soul cries out
My heart is scrambling for cover
There's no place to hide
in the warmth of your gaze
You see my truth exposed
broken and bare
So I bask in your light
whole

-November 2011

Inspiration

A mark on my soul
Indelible, inappropriate, inspiring
Forever changed
Intense, irresistible, impossible

-December 2011

First Time Last Times

Everyone thinks about
the first breath
first words
first laugh

And I remember your first day of TK
you walked away
It was the first of the
Last times of you needing me to
kiss a knee
climb a tree
read to me
Oh, we don't remember the first time, last times

Do you remember your
first crush
first team
first game
first dreams

I remember your first day of 9th grade
you turned away
It was the first of the
Last times of you wanting me
in the stands
at the dance
hold your hand
Oh, we don't remember the first time, last times

And now you're thinking of your
first dance
first chance
first car
first kiss

But I keep thinking of your last day of 12th grade
you drove away
It was the first of the
Last times of you needing me
I prayed
please stay
come back to me
I know why we don't remember the first time, last times

Now my sweet boy
Is a grown man
With a strong faith
And a good woman

And now your son just took
his first breath
first step
first words
first laugh

I will love you with my
whole heart
arms wide
Last breath
One day it'll be the last time for the first times.

-October 2019

The Grace of God

Start the day on bended knee
Too late, there is no time
When I remember, I forget
Amnesia of the spirit kind.

Your mercy is a boundless sea
And yet I choke, I grasp
Forsaking all your soothing rest
Quench my thirst on broken glass.

Chasing after darkness
I turn away, I shun
Craving pale mirages
Over the radiance of your Son.

But the grace of God, it finds me
My traitor heart, my soul
Surrendered to my brokenness
By Him, I am made whole.

-January 2021

www.ingramcontent.com/pod-product-compliance
Lightning Source LLC
Chambersburg PA
CBHW020959090426
42736CB00010B/1385